THE GREAT BOOK OF ANIMAL KNOWLEDGE

WALRUSES

Tusked Arctic Giants

Introduction

Walruses are huge, flabby marine mammals. They can be found in groups in the icy cold arctic waters. The body of a walrus is built to survive the extreme cold. Walruses are also very good swimmers.

What Walruses Look Like

Photo by claumoho (flickr.com/claudiah), as licensed under CC BY 2.0 Generic

Walruses are huge animals. They look very similar to seals. There are a few differences but the main difference is that walruses have two giant tusks extending from their mouth.

Size and Weight

Walruses can grow almost 12 feet long! And they are also very, very heavy animals. They weigh 1.5 tons!! That's 3000 pounds! Walruses are one of the heaviest animals in the world.

Where Walruses Live

Walruses live in very cold parts of the world. They can be found in the northernmost parts of the arctic and pacific oceans. Walruses can survive the extreme cold temperatures there because they are well adapted to it.

Skin

Photo by Rojer (flickr.com/rojer), as licensed under CC BY 2.0 Generic

The skin of a walrus is very thick and wrinkled. It can be almost 4 inches thick around the neck of a walrus. Walruses have sparse fur around their bodies and their skin can change color. When walruses go underwater, their skin appears whitish, and when they are resting where there is sunlight they appear to be pinkish.

Blubber

Under a walruses skin is a thick layer of fat called blubber. This layer of blubber can sometimes be 6 inches thick and can cover about 1/3 of a walrus' body mass! Blubber helps walruses survive the extremely cold temperatures of the arctic.

Movement

Photo by claumoho (flickr.com/claudiah), as licensed under CC BY 2.0 Generic

Walruses spend more time on water than on land. Their flippers make it easy for them to swim and move around under water. On land, however, walruses have a harder time moving around because they are so heavy and their body shape is designed for movements in the water.

Flippers

Walruses use their flippers to navigate easily under water. When on land, walruses use their front flippers to pull themselves around. Walruses also use their front flippers for scratching themselves when they itch.

Tusks

Walruses are known for their two huge tusks. These tusks are actually teeth. Walruses use their tusks to pull themselves out of the water and into the land. They also use it to chip out ice when they need to. Tusks are also used for fighting each other and predators.

Groups

Photo by Smudge 9000 (flickr.com/smudge9000), as licensed under CC BY-SA 2.0 Generic

Walruses are very social animals. It is very rare to see a walrus alone with no other walruses nearby. They live in groups called herds. There are male herds and female herds. A group of walruses changes over time with some members leaving and new ones joining.

Sounds

Walruses make many different sounds. These sounds include grunting, barking and whistling. When males confront each other they usually roar, snort or cough. Male walruses can also make sounds underwater. It is believed that this underwater communication helps them find each other.

Breeding

The walrus breeding season is from December to March. Female walruses that are ready to mate separate themselves from pregnant females and form a group. Walruses are noisy during the mating season. Males make these noises to get the attention of a female they want to mate with and to warn other males to stay away.

Fighting Each Other

Photo by claumoho (flickr.com/claudiah), as licensed under CC BY 2.0 Generic

Males get very aggressive during the mating season. They will sometimes fight each other for the right to mate. Walruses fight each other with their tusks, and sometimes these fights results in the death of one.

Baby Walrus

Photo by Kai Schreiber (flickr.com/genista), as licensed under CC BY-SA 2.0 Generic

Female walruses give birth about 16 months after mating. Newborn walruses already weight 100-160 pounds! They can swim right away and will follow their mother when she goes to the water. Baby walruses drink their mother's milk for 1 year.

Life of a Walrus

Photo by Polar Cruises (flickr.com/polarphotos), as licensed under CC BY 2.0 Generic

At six months old walruses will start eating other foods besides their mother's milk. Young walruses stay with their mother for two years unless she has a new baby. Male walruses are mature at 8 years old but they usually don't mate until they reach 15 years old. Females are mature at 6 but don't mate until they reach 10. Walruses can live up to 40 years old.

What Walruses Eat

Photo by Quinn Dombrowski (flickr.com/quinnanya), as licensed under CC BY-SA 2.0 Generic

Walruses are carnivores; they hunt and eat other animals. Walruses feed on clams, shrimps, crabs, and sometimes even birds and dead seals!

How Walruses Eat

Photo by Quinn Dombrowski (flickr.com/quinnanya), as licensed under CC BY-SA 2.0 Generic

Walruses dive to the sea floor to search for food there. They can stay underwater for up to 30 minutes! Walruses use their sensitive whiskers to search for food. Once they find a clam, they will put it in their mouth and suck the soft part out of the shell then drop the hard parts on the sea floor. Walruses need a lot of food every day; they can eat lots of clams in just a few minutes!

Migration

Although some groups of walruses stay in one area all year round, many groups migrate. They migrate north during the summer when the ice melts in the southern areas, and they go back south when the ice freezes again.

Predators

Because walruses are so huge and have long dangerous tusks, they only have a few predators. Their only predators are the polar bear and killer whale. Their predators hunt for young or weak walruses. Fighting a healthy adult walrus is too dangerous for the predator. Parasites also sometimes live in walruses and can kill their host.

Endangered

Photo by kerryinlondon (flickr.com/kerrylondon), as licensed under CC BY 2.0 Generic

Walruses were once heavily hunted for the ivory in their tusks, oil from their blubber, and their meat. Today, only Native Americans in some locations can hunt walruses legally. This is because the natives rely on the walrus for food and many other needs. Global warming is also affecting walruses. Walruses spend a lot of time in the ice, and as the ice slowly melts away the walrus will have nowhere to stay!

Relatives

Photo by Alan (flickr.com/adavey), as licensed under CC BY 2.0 Generic

True seals and sea lions are the closest relatives to walruses. They look quite similar and they are both marine mammals. Polar bears, otters, and badgers are also distant relatives to walruses.

Get the next book in this series!

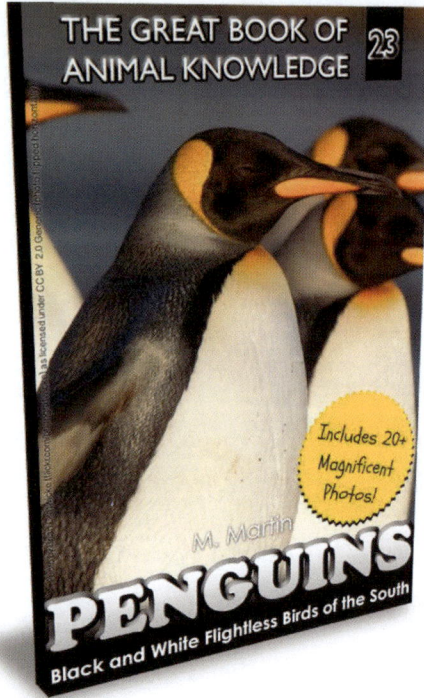

THE GREAT BOOK OF ANIMAL KNOWLEDGE 23

Includes 20+ Magnificent Photos!

M. Martin

PENGUINS

Black and White Flightless Birds of the South

PENGUINS: Black and White Flightless Birds of the South

Log on to Facebook.com/GazelleCB for more info

Tip: Use the key-phrase "The Great Book of Animal Knowledge" when searching for books in this series.

GAZELLE
CHILDREN'S BOOKS

For more information about our
books, discounts and updates,
please Like us on FaceBook!

Facebook.com/GazelleCB

Printed in Great Britain
by Amazon